The 1759 Battle of Quebec: The History and Legacy of Britain's Most Important Victory of the French & Indian War

By Charles River Editors

Benjamin West's painting of General Wolfe during the battle

About Charles River Editors

Charles River Editors provides superior editing and original writing services across the digital publishing industry, with the expertise to create digital content for publishers across a vast range of subject matter. In addition to providing original digital content for third party publishers, we also republish civilization's greatest literary works, bringing them to new generations of readers via ebooks.

Sign up here to receive updates about free books as we publish them, and visit Our Kindle Author Page to browse today's free promotions and our most recently published Kindle titles.

Introduction

A contemporary depiction of the battle

The Battle of Quebec

"[W]e observed the Enemy marching down towards us in three Columns, at 10 they formed their Line of Battle, which was at least six deep, having their Flanks covered by a thick Wood on each Side, into which they threw above 3000 Canadians and Indians, who gauled us much; the Regulars then marched briskly up to us, and gave us their first Fire, at about Fifty Yards Distance, which we did not return, as it was General Wolfe's express Orders not to fire till they came within twenty Yards of us…" – The British Sergeant-Major of Gen. Hopson's Grenadiers

On September 13, 1759, a battle was fought on the Plains of Abraham outside the old city of Québec that was one of the turning point battles in world history. Thanks to the British victory and the events that followed, Canada went from being a colony of France (New France) to being a colony of Great Britain, which permanently changed Canadian history. In many ways, the outcome of the battle brought about several American attempts to seize Canada during the Revolutionary War and War of 1812, and ultimately it ensured that when Canada became an independent country, it was part of the British Commonwealth with an Anglophone majority and a Francophone minority. Frictions over cultural and political issues between the English Canadians and the Québécois, dating back to the battle, continue to impact the state of affairs in Canada today.

While the battle had a profound impact, it has also been romanticized and mythologized beyond even epic proportions. Though often forgotten today (more than 250 years after the battle), the Battle of the Plains of Abraham was the culmination of a long siege, and the decisive action itself was an incredibly short affair at less than half an hour. Despite that brevity, both commanding generals were mortally wounded in the exchange, making British General James Wolfe a national hero on both sides of the Atlantic and French General Louis-Joseph de Montcalm a convenient scapegoat. Only a few thousand soldiers were engaged on each side, and the battle ended with less than 1,500 casualties combined.

Regardless, the French were compelled to quit Quebec after the battle, giving up one of their most important colonial possessions in the New World, and when the fighting ended in North America in 1760, the British still held the city. When the Seven Years War ended on the European continent, the subsequent treaty forced the French to cede most of their North American possessions to the British, and it also left Britain in tough economic straits, which would set about a chain of events that brought about the American Revolution in the following decade.

The 1759 Battle of Quebec: The History and Legacy of Britain's Most Important Victory of the French & Indian War looks at the campaign that culminated with the pivotal battle of the French & Indian War. Along with pictures of important people, places, and events, you will learn about the Battle of Quebec like never before, in no time at all.

The 1759 Battle of Quebec: The History and Legacy of Britain's Most Important Victory of the French & Indian War

About Charles River Editors

Introduction

    Chapter 1: New France

    Chapter 2: The Struggle for North America

    Chapter 3: The Seven Years War

    Chapter 4: The Battle of Québec

    Chapter 5: Aftermath of the Battle

    Chapter 6: The Legacy of the Battle and the War

    Bibliography

Chapter 1: New France

The French first staked their territorial claim in North America under the realm of King Francis I, starting with the voyage of Giovanni da Verrazano in 1524 and the voyages of Jacques Cartier in the 1530s. Verrazano cruised the east coast of what is now the United States and Canada, and a few years later, Cartier made the first of three trips to the New World. On his first voyage in 1534, Cartier explored Newfoundland, the Gaspé Peninsula, and the Gulf of St. Lawrence, which he hoped might lead to a Northwest Passage through the North American landmass to China and its trade riches.

Cartier

Verrazano

During his first trip, Cartier and his men planted a cross on the Gaspé Peninsula, claiming the region for France, but the French had encounters there with the inhabitants already on the land: the Micmacs and the Iroquoians. Cartier returned again the next year, and this time he went up the St. Lawrence, where he visited the Iroquoian villages of Stadacona and Hochelaga located on the sites of Québec City and Montreal respectively. Both are strategic locations on the river, with Québec at the point where the river narrows with a commanding promontory on the northern bank and Montreal at the point where the river has a major set of rapids preventing further ascent without portages. At the request of the king, Cartier made a third voyage to

Canada in 1541, but his attempt to plant a colony on the St. Lawrence River with settlers miscarried.

Due to violent religious conflicts and power struggles in France between Catholics and Protestants (Huguenots), the French crown was unable to follow-up on Cartier's discoveries until the early 17th century. In 1604, the French tried to establish a colony on an island in the St. Croix River, the present-day boundary between the Maine and New Brunswick, but that effort lasted only one hard winter. Seeking out a better place, they removed the next year to Port Royal on the Annapolis Basin, a large ocean inlet, in what is now Nova Scotia. Attacked by an English force in 1613, this was abandoned and then reoccupied later by the French (to be held onto by the French until another war with the English in 1710).

In the meantime, a French settlement farther away from further possible English attacks and nearer to what was still thought might well be a passage leading to the Orient was established at Québec in 1608. Québec became the capital of New France, and shiploads of French settlers slowly arrived. Small farming settlements spread out along the St. Lawrence River east and west of Québec as well.

The main figure in the successful French colonization of Canada was Samuel de Champlain, who had also participated in the voyages that looked along the Atlantic coast for a suitable French place to settle. In fact, establishing a trading post and settlement at Québec was his idea, due in part to the fact that by the early 17th century, the Iroquoian village of Stadacona had mysteriously disappeared. Champlain was also the man who made friends with many of the Algonquian-speaking Indian tribes, an important factor that enabled the French to hold onto their colony for as long as they did by offsetting in wars the advantage in population enjoyed by the English colonies along the eastern seaboard. At the highest point of Québec overlooking the river where Champlain had built a fort in 1620, there is now a large bronze statue of him flanked by cannons honoring his achievements.

George Agnew Reid's painting of Champlain landing near Quebec

The bronze statue of Champlain in Quebec

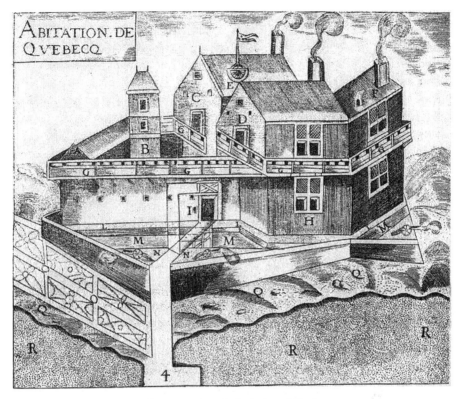

A 17th century French depiction of Quebec

Québec remained small during its time as a French possession, existing as little more than a large village, and it had just 8,000 inhabitants at the time of its conquest by the British in 1759. Initially, the settlement occupied a narrow strip next to the river where the port was located, and this "Lower Town" was where merchants had their shops and warehouses, particularly for the fur trade in beaver pelts that became New France's economic mainstay. Along with the activities and employment attendant on being a seat of government for the colony, Québec became a base of missionary efforts by the Jesuits directed at the Indians. An "Upper Town" developed with the growth of government and the needs of the Church for building space.

A depiction of Quebec in 1800

A Swedish traveler, Peter Kalm, described his impressions of Québec on his visit in 1749: "Quebec lies on the western shore of the river St. Lawrence, close to the water's edge, on a neck of land bounded by that river on the east side, and by the river St. Charles on the north side; the mountain on which the town is built rises still higher on the south side, and behind it begin great pastures; and the same mountain likewise extends a good way westward. The city is distinguished into the lower and the upper town. The lower lies on the river, eastward of the upper. The neck of land mentioned before, was formed by the dirt and filth which had from time to time been accumulated there, and by a rock which lay that way, not by any gradual diminution of the water. The upper city lies above the other, on a high hill, and takes up five or six times the space of the lower, though it is not quite so populous. The mountain on which the upper city is situated, reaches above the houses of the lower city. Notwithstanding the latter are three or four stories high, and the view, from the palace, of the lower city, is enough to cause a swimming of the head. There is only one easy way of getting to the upper city, and there part of the mountain has been blown up. This road is very steep, notwithstanding it is made winding and serpentine. However, they go up and down it in carriages and with wagons. All the other roads up the mountain are so steep, that it is very difficult to climb to the top of them. Most of the merchants live in the lower city, where the houses are built very close together. The streets in it are narrow, very rugged, and almost always wet. The upper city is inhabited by people of quality, by several persons belonging to the different offices, by tradesmen and others. In this part are the chief buildings of the town."

Québec's Upper Town was defended on two sides by precipices and steep slopes falling off to the St. Charles River along the north and the St. Lawrence River along the south. On the west side, facing the open countryside where the city was vulnerable to attack, a wooden wall with gates was built in 1690 and then extended and strengthened with masonry in 1745. Inside the wall was the governor's palace, the attendant's house, the cathedral, a convent, and the oldest hospital north of Mexico. Soldiers were housed in the four-story Dauphine Redoubt, built to withstand enemy bombardments and located in the northwest part of the wall.

Three times prior to 1759, attacking English forces had tried to capture Québec, and only the first attempt in 1629 was successful when the English adventurer David Kirke forced the surrender of a starving Québec through the interdiction of the flow of supplies that were brought by ships from France. However, Québec was given back to control of the French a few years later during the peace negotiations that ended the Anglo-French War. In 1690, during King William's War, an expedition from New England under Sir William Phips landed militia troops at Beauport on the St. Lawrence northeast of Québec, hoping to attack the city from that beachhead. The governor, Count Frontenac, strengthened the city's defenses, Canadian militia and Indians harassed the English landing party, and cannons firing down from the city wrecked the English ships. With their soldiers also dying from smallpox, the English left the city in defeat. A third English attempt in 1711 during Queen Anne's War ended in disaster before it even got anywhere close to the city. Shipwrecks on the north shore of the St. Lawrence drowned 850 of the soldiers en route, and the expedition had to be abandoned.

During King George's War (1744-1748), the big French fortress at Louisbourg on Cape Breton, which protected the shipping lanes to New France, was captured by a New England expedition. However, Québec was not attacked, in no small part to the fact it had gained a reputation for being an impregnable city.

That reputation would be tested in the next war.

Chapter 2: The Struggle for North America

In order to understand the significance of the Battle of Québec in 1759, it's necessary to understand what the French Annales historians have called the "longue durée." Specifically, that means going back to the early 17th century and the struggle between France and England (subsequently Great Britain) that lasted throughout the establishment of both sides' first permanent colonies in North America. The two European rivals fought a series of wars which all had certain European causes but were also fought in the New World in order to determine which power would control North America. Naturally, the French and English colonists fought each other, often with the involvement of troops that came from Europe.

In 1607, the year before the French established Québec, the English had established their first permanent colony in North America -- which they named Jamestown after their king – on the estuary of the James River in Virginia. The Virginia colony nearly failed before stability was found in the form of tobacco, which was produced on plantations and farms using the work of indentured servants and enslaved Africans. The next permanent English colonies to be established were religious in nature; the Pilgrims came to the area of Cape Cod in 1620 to find a place where they could practice their own version of Protestantism, a denomination being persecuted back in England. They established Plymouth Plantation, and they were followed in 1629 by the Puritans, who had a similar theology but wanted to create a "City on a Hill" to inspire the people left behind in England. They established Boston and nearby towns in the Massachusetts Bay Colony. Unlike the Virginia colony, which consisted mostly of young men seeking their fortunes, the Pilgrims and Puritans brought whole families with them.

More English colonies soon followed: Maryland, another tobacco colony, was established in 1633, and Connecticut (another Puritan colony) and Rhode Island (established by the dissident Puritan clergyman Roger Williams) were established in 1636. New Hampshire was established by land speculators in 1638.

During the 1640s and 1650s, England was torn apart by a civil war between Anglicans and Puritans, and after the king was beheaded, the nation was run by Puritans as a Commonwealth. After the restoration of the monarchy in 1660, more English colonies in America were founded, including North Carolina (1653), South Carolina (1663), New Jersey (1664), and Pennsylvania (1682). The Dutch colony of New Netherlands was seized by war in 1664 and transformed into the English colony of New York, and Georgia was founded in 1732.

Populations in these English colonies grew quite rapidly. Including both persons of European and African descent, populations in the English colonies rose from under 5,000 in 1630 to over 250,000 by 1700 and 1,200,000 in 1750. The population grew rapidly in part because people, especially in the New England colonies, lived longer in a more salubrious environment, and with more available land on which to set up farms than in the Old World, young people could marry sooner. Thus, a woman was able to bear more children in the New World; in New England, having 8 or 10 children was not unusual. More stable families were also established in the tobacco colonies thanks to the arrival of more women, while Pennsylvania attracted immigrants from Germany and elsewhere because it was run by pacifist Quakers who were tolerant of religious differences. These immigrants also had large farm families, and more land was needed with each succeeding generation to set up farms.

New France expanded territorially during this same time period, and its expansion was driven by two principal factors, one being the fur trade and the other being the work of the missionaries among the Indians. Montreal was founded in 1642 and took over some of the role of Québec as a fur trading center, and in 1673, Louis Jolliet and Jesuit Father Jacques Marquette explored the upper Mississippi and Ohio Rivers, subsequently establishing a French claim to that whole region (from which both beaver pelts and human souls were collected). In 1682, a party led by fur trader Robert de La Salle descended the Illinois River, went all the way down the Mississippi, and claimed Louisiana for the King of France, Louis XIV. A French settlement at New Orleans was founded in 1718.

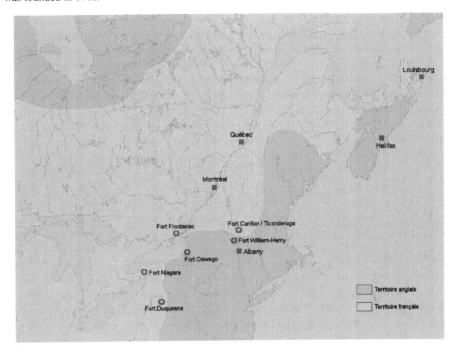

A map of French and English forts in the 18th century

With a small white population due to a much lower rate of immigration and a lower birth rate, the need for more land to raise crops was not an impetus for the French expansion like it was with the English colonies. Thus, despite claiming a vast amount of territory stretching from the frigid North Atlantic and the St. Lawrence to the balmy Gulf of Mexico, there were very few French people other than in a handful of places like Québec. In 1685, New France had a population of little more than 20,000 (compared to 160,000 in New England), and at the time of the French & Indian War, the population of New France was no more than 75,000. The French government occasionally tried to encourage immigration, but news of Canada's harsh winters, which made farming a challenge, made such a sale difficult. Early on, there was a shortage of women in the colony, and it was not fully remedied even after the French government shipped over 800 young, marriageable women between 1663 and 1673. As an alternative, many French men took on a native lifestyle, becoming *coureurs des bois* (literally, runners in the woods), working in the fur trade, and marrying Indian women. In general, better French connections with the Indians helped to partially offset the growing disparity in population with the English-speaking colonies.

Thus, by the early 18th century, there were a total of 13 colonies along the East Coast of North America, and their burgeoning populations were already beginning to press up against the Appalachian Mountain barrier. Enclosing them on the north and the west was a lightly populated New France whose existence hampered further English expansion. This was a situation with great potential for conflicts to happen, and it was exacerbated by the religious tensions between the Puritans of New England and the Catholics of Canada. For instance, in 1724, Massachusetts militia undertook an expedition to eliminate the French priest Father Rale who was doing missionary work among the Abenaki Indians in Maine and was encouraging them to attack the Protestant "heretics."

That said, the main cause of conflict between the French and the English settlers in the North America colonies was simply the fact that the two ambitious powers were constantly fighting in Europe. When they fought against each other on the other side of the Atlantic, they also fought each other in the New World. As a result, it could be said that the Seven Years War (1756-63), remembered in North America as the French & Indian War, was an exception of sorts because instead of starting in Europe and then spreading to North America, it started in the New World.

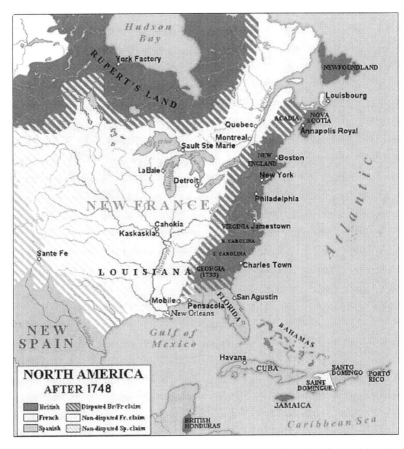

A map of the French and British colonial possessions, as well as the disputed territories

Chapter 3: The Seven Years War

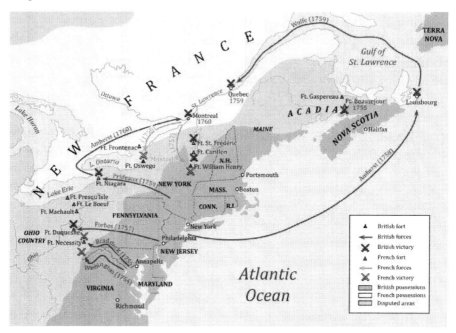

A map of important forts and sites of battle during the French & Indian War

The flames of what became a huge global contest between Great Britain and France for dominance were lit in 1753 over conflicting claims to the Ohio territory west of the Appalachian Mountains, and ironically, it prominently involved a young Virginian named George Washington. The French had set up Fort Duquesne at the site of present-day Pittsburgh, where the Allegheny and Monongahela Rivers come together to make the Ohio River, and the British contested it. Virginia's Governor, Robert Dinwiddie, was familiar with the Washington family due to Lawrence Washington's position in the Virginia militia, and he had appointed George to the rank of major in the Virginia militia after Lawrence's death. With the French building fortresses on land the British claimed as their own, the British authorities decided to step in by delivering a letter to the French demanding that they withdraw from British land. It was Washington who volunteered to carry a letter from the governor of Virginia to the French commander of the forts recently built.

George Washington

Dinwiddie

Washington used his expedition as an opportunity to further both Britain's fortunes and his own. In the journal he kept, Washington describes how he practiced diplomacy to keep the Native leaders allied to the British cause, as well as how he interviewed French deserters. With his background in land surveying, he reported on the extent of French military posts between New Orleans and the Great Lakes, and he skillfully reconnoitered the Forks of the Ohio with an eye to the proper site for building a fort. He even went so far as to inspect and report on the construction of the new French forts, and he made estimates of their strength and preparations for the following year's expeditions. All of this information would come in handy when Washington and the British found themselves in the midst of a border dispute over that same territory the following year, ultimately triggering the French & Indian War.

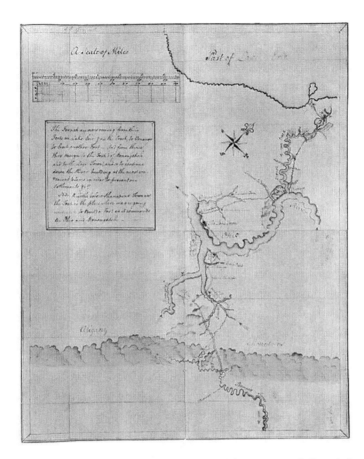

A map of the Ohio River Valley drawn by Washington to mark French forts

Washington delivered the ultimatum, but it was not well received. The note demanded that the French abandon their positions in Ohio, but the French's construction of forts made it clear they were hardly interested in moving. Washington delivered the message in December of 1753, but hostilities between the two empires would break out in early 1754. At the same time, Washington's journal of his journey was reprinted throughout the colonies and became popular reading throughout the Empire.

In the 1750s, Virginia's colonial military was the most important among the British imperial military units in the New World, and Major Washington's actions had received notoriety across the colonies and in London. Thus, when the French didn't back down, Washington was a natural choice to lead a small group to head back to the region and defend it, for which he was also promoted to Lieutenant Colonel.

As it turned out, Washington was at the head of a debacle that led to the outbreak of fighting on the continent. In an event that is still controversial and in dispute, Washington's small group happened upon a detachment of French troops in Pennsylvania and attacked them, killing the leader of the French group, Joseph Coulon de Jumonville. The French were outraged at what they claimed was an ambush of a non-military contingent, and in July 1754 a French unit attacked the fort that Washington's men were constructing, Fort Necessity, capturing Washington in the process.

When Washington surrendered to the French, he signed the capitulation in French, a language he did not understand, stating that England had trespassed into French territory and would not return for a year. Despite his role in these embarrassing events, Washington made lemonade out of lemons. In fact, his celebrity on both sides of the Atlantic increased when he issued a written description of the Battle of Fort Necessity, which fascinated readers in the colonies and in England. He was promoted to Colonel, and he would be on the front lines fighting the French for control of Ohio shortly thereafter.

Some historians have called the Seven Years War the first true World War, and they make a good point. In Europe, an alliance of Great Britain, the German state of Hanover (the ruling house of Britain was from Hanover) and Prussia fought a series of battles against an alliance of France, Austria and Russia, with the occasional involvement of some other European powers such as Sweden and Spain. The war was also fought in many other parts of the world, including in India, West Africa and the Caribbean, where both the French and the British had colonies. In addition to the fighting on land, battles were fought between ships on the high seas, and these naval battles were generally won by the British, who boasted the 18th century's best navy.

The standard infantry weapon used by all sides during the Seven Years War was the smoothbore flintlock musket. The British had the famous Brown Bess musket, which was still in use during the Napoleonic Wars, and bayonets could be affixed to the muskets to turn them into pikes. After one or two volleys, armies typically closed on each other with bayonets.

In the intervals between wars, many hours were spent in drilling paid professional soldiers so that they could operate in units like clockwork at the command of their officers without faltering as they were being fired at. Conversely, in North America, almost all able-bodied males from the ages of 16-60 were members of the colonial militia, whose numbers were called out to supplement the professionals. Militia members were poorly-armed and trained, turning out once or twice a year on the town green for a muster day before retiring quickly to the nearby tavern for refreshment. They might not stand in battle, but their numbers could be useful.

An 18th century depiction of a soldier holding a Brown Bess

Field artillery used during this time period could fire iron cannon balls weighing up to 9-12 pounds or be loaded with an agglomeration of small round lead balls ("grapeshot"). The latter could be devastating at close range on ranks or columns of advancing soldiers.

The French & Indian War was directly impacted by the war raging in Europe and elsewhere in several different ways: The more pressing need for soldiers and sailors to fight elsewhere in this far-flung conflict meant that reinforcements were not always available to be sent to America. This was especially a problem for France, which was located on the European continent and was practically surrounded by enemies on all sides. For that reason, the French needed to maintain a large army at home, but this was less of a problem for Great Britain, which did not need a large standing army thanks to the Atlantic and the English Channel. The ability to send reinforcements and supplies to North America was also contingent on whether ships could get through without being interdicted by the enemy, which posed problems for both sides but especially the French.

In North America, military tactics were also somewhat less rigid. The French in particular had become adept at fighting "Indian-style," launching guerilla attacks and raids alongside their Indian allies. Indians armed with muskets fought well at times, but they also had different motives for fighting; they were fighting for the glory of acquiring captives, not so much for the purpose of defeating the enemy altogether and taking over their old territory.

The Seven Years War was inconclusive for the first several years, but it started rather badly for the British. In July 1755, Major General Edward Braddock, with Washington as an aide, set out with one of the largest units in the colonies for the Ohio River Valley in an effort to take the region from the French. Instead, the expedition was a disaster, and eventually Braddock's expedition was permanently set back by its loss at the Battle of Monongahela. Braddock was killed in the fighting, and while this was seen as a devastating defeat for the British, Washington survived unscathed and was lauded as a hero for rallying troops as they retreated in disorder.

The following year went poorly for the British as well, though the war only technically became official when Britain declared war on France on May 8, 1756. Just a few weeks later in May, the French fleet defeated a British fleet and captured the strategic island of Minorca in the Mediterranean, where the British had a garrison. The admiral of the British fleet was subsequently court-martialed and executed by a firing squad. A few months later, the French took Fort Oswego on Lake Ontario in August 1756 after 1,700 British soldiers surrendered.

The British ruling establishment in London was thrown into a state of turmoil by these events, and their savior was William Pitt the Elder, an eloquent orator in Parliament who had been a severe critic of the previous government. Pitt came to power for the first time late in 1756 by promising to do whatever it took to turn the tide of war against France. In Europe, Pitt's strategy called for heavily supporting allies like Prussia with monetary subsidies so that they could do the fighting instead of British soldiers there. While the French were tied down with the fighting on the continent, the British would use their powerful navy to go after them in other parts of the world and push Britain's own imperial and mercantilist interests. In North America, Pitt urged the colonial legislatures to appropriate funds for the recruitment of large numbers of troops while promising that the British would help to pay for it. A new set of young officers were also sent to take over the leadership from those who had failed, and Pitt himself took a hands-on approach to strategy.

William Pitt the Elder

All these commitments by Pitt led to heavy indebtedness on the part of the Crown, which would bring about some unanticipated consequences within the 13 colonies down the road, but at the time, they began to show immediate results. In the summer of 1758, several British expeditionary forces sent to West Africa captured the French fort at Saint-Louis in Senegal, their fort on the island of Gorée, and a French slave-trading factory on the River Gambia. These victories brought back shiploads of riches that would have otherwise helped fund the French war effort. A naval expedition was sent to the Caribbean to try to capture the rich French sugar plantation islands there, and though it failed to capture Martinique, it did manage to capture Guadeloupe.

Meanwhile, there was progress in North America during that year too. While things did not go well for the British in their attempts to advance on French Canada via the Champlain Valley, they did capture Fortress Louisbourg on Cape Breton, paving the way for a campaign against Québec during the following year's fighting season. Fort Duquesne was also taken over from the French and renamed Fort Pitt.

An engraving that depicts the capture of Fort Duquesne

In the great colonial prize of India, the British made progress against their French rivals. At the Battle of Plassey on June 23, 1757, the British East India Company, acting on its own, had administered a defeat to the Nawab of Bengal, who was supported by the French East India Company. This became the turning point for British control of India; although part of India was returned to France at the end of the war, the British eventually ousted them from India altogether.

For the French government, the main area of importance was continental Europe, with the colonies being peripheral. The British navy, which outnumbered the French navy in ships by a ratio of about three to one, made resupply from France to Canada difficult, so New France was mostly left on its own. As such, for the French Canadians, their war had to be a defensive one in nature; lacking sufficient manpower, there was never any thought of attacking and capturing British cities like Boston or New York.

In addition to a defensive stance, the many Indian allies of the French could be used to make raids on the frontier settlements to keep the colonists off balance, much the same way they were used in the previous wars fought between the French and the British in North America. Furthermore, they could be deployed in battle to supplement regular troops, which had the added advantage of instilling fear in British soldiers who worried about being captured and tortured to death by Indians.

To a degree, the French prosecuted the war under the assumption that even if parts of New France were lost to the British during the war, the French government could have them restored during the subsequent tradeoffs made in the peace negotiations. After all, Fortress Louisbourg had been given back to France at the end of King George's War despite being taken from them in 1745.

It was against this backdrop that the Battle of Québec was fought on September 13, 1759, the war's fifth year in America.

Chapter 4: The Battle of Québec

After their early embarrassing defeats by the French and Indians from 1755-1758, the British were determined to commit enough soldiers and resources to beat the French in North America once and for all. This meant that Québec, with its strategic location on the St. Lawrence River controlling the flow of commerce from the Great Lakes and the interior of New France, was vital to British strategy. 9,000 soldiers were assigned to do what the British had been unable to do in 1690 and 1711: capture the city and turn it into a British fortress.

Commanding the British land forces was 32-year old James Wolfe, a veteran of the War of the Austrian Succession (known as "King George's War" in America) who had also participated in the Battle of Culloden in Scotland (which dashed the hopes of Bonnie Prince Charlie). When the Seven Years War began, he saw some action in an unsuccessful attack on the coast of France, but after being sent to America in 1758 as a Brigadier General, Wolfe took part in the successful capture of Fortress Louisbourg under the command of Maj. Gen. Jeffrey Amherst. Wolfe also had capable officers under him, including Robert Monckton as his second-in-command, while the British naval commander of the Québec expedition was Admiral Charles Saunders, a veteran naval officer since 1727 who had fought previously with the Mediterranean fleet.

Wolfe

Monckton

Saunders

The commanding officer in charge of the French defenses at Québec was the Marquis de Montcalm, who was 47 years old and had been part of the French military since the age of 12. Montcalm had also served during the War of the Austrian Succession, during which he was severely wounded and taken prisoner, but after the war, he lived life as a provincial nobleman. In 1756, he was appointed to replace Baron de Dieskau, the French military commander in America who had been captured by the British during fighting in 1755, yet he had somewhat limited authority; the governor-general of the colony, Pierre de Rigaud de Vaudreuil, was the commander-in-chief, so Montcalm was only in charge of operations in the field. Despite being occasionally at odds with the Canadian-born Vaudreuil, and having fewer soldiers at his disposal than the British did, Montcalm nonetheless adeptly executed Vaudreuil's plans and prevented a

British invasion of Canada from the south in 1757 and 1758. At Fort William Henry on Lake George and at Fort Carillon on Lake Champlain, the British and American colonial militia were twice beaten badly by 4,000 French regulars and their colonial militia and Indian allies.

Montcalm

Pierre de Rigaud de Vaudreuil

Montcalm, thoroughly schooled in the European school of warfare, was not pleased with the less-regimented form of warfare he found in America. He was leery of undisciplined militia and Indians, whereas the Canadian-born Vaudreuil knew of their value. However, as the historian William R. Nester has observed, "The fifth war for North America was unlike any that preceded it. In his three years in Canada, General Montcalm found that the 'nature of war in this colony has totally changed. Formerly the Canadians thought they were making war when they went on raids resembling hunting-parties – now we have formal operations; formerly the Indians were the basis of thing, now they are only auxiliaries. We now need other views, other principles. I say this; but the old principles remain.' Montcalm's aid, Louis de Bouganville, also noticed the change: 'Now war is established here on the European basis. It is no longer a matter of making a raid, but of conquering or being conquered. What a revolution!'"

Although the nature of warfare in North America was often different, the siege and battle for Québec would fought largely on European lines. The British plan for 1759 was to invade the French Canadian heartland simultaneously on three different fronts: in the west in Ohio and on the Great Lakes, a thrust along the Champlain Valley, and up the St. Lawrence to Québec from the newly-captured Louisbourg. For his part, Montcalm had a realistic understanding of the daunting task he was up against; he was pessimistic about being able to defeat the British attacks but felt resistance was necessary in order to uphold the honor of the French military. Thus, in early 1759, Montcalm and other Canadian leaders met and adopted a defensive strategy, and this is also what the French government, which could spare no reinforcements, advocated in the hopes that parts of Canada could be retained and the rest recovered at the peace talks to end what was now a global war. If the British appeared with overwhelming force, a delaying action would be fought in the Champlain Valley with the French forces falling back to the top of the lake, and meanwhile, a force was sent above the Montreal rapids to protect it from the direction of Lake Ontario. Canadians were exhorted to come to the defense of their *patrie* and their Catholic religion.

Boosting confidence at Québec, most of the ships in a supply convoy sent from France had managed to slip by the watchful British ships and reach the city in May 1759. Upon learning that a British expedition had gathered and was on its way to try to conquer Québec, Montcalm and Vaudreuil hurried from Montreal to organize the defenses, and most of the rest of the Canadian armed forces were concentrated there as well. The city's defensive force was not insubstantial; the professional core of it consisted of eight battalions of regular infantry (*Troupes de Terre*) from France numbering some 3,685 men, along with two battalions of Marine Independent Companies *(Compagnies Franches de la Marine)*. Also present at Québec were considerable numbers of less well-trained Canadian militia, including 5,640 men from the Québec militia, 5,455 from the Montreal militia, 1,100 from Trois-Rivière, and over 1,000 Indians.

The British fleet approaching the city was a sizable one consisting of 320 ships, including 49 warships, 55 troop transports, 2 hospital ships and 134 landing craft. Aboard were more than 9,000 British and American professional soldiers, plus approximately 2,100 sailors and soldiers of the Royal Marines. In addition, there were 600 American irregulars known as "rangers." Canadians hoped the British ships would have trouble navigating the treacherous waters of the St. Lawrence, and that the same fate might happen to them as had befallen the shipwrecked British expedition in 1711, but to prevent that from happening, the British took captive several French river pilots and gave them the blunt choice of showing them the right way or being hanged from a ship's yardarm. On June 21st, the sails of the first British ships could be seen from Québec while anchored off the île d'Orléans. Led by a party of 40 rangers, one of whom was killed and scalped by the Indians, British soldiers landed and occupied the island on June 27th. After that, the whole army was landed there and encamped at the extreme western point of the island. The island had been deserted by the French, with the rector or curate of the parish leaving a note behind imploring the British soldiers to respect his church and not to do damage to it. Almost immediately, the British soldiers started plundering the abandoned farmhouses there.

Anticipating a British landing on the north shore of the St. Lawrence to the east of the city, Montcalm directed most of his forces as they arrived on the scene to be stationed between the St.

Charles River and the Montmorency River with its large spectacular waterfall. Here they dug trenches, built redoubts and set up batteries with a second line of defenses behind it closer to the city. The mouth of the St. Charles River was closed off with a log boom and protected by cannons mounted on two hulks. A bridge of boats across the river connected this shore in the *ville* of Beauport with the city, and the walls of the city mounted over 100 cannons. On the river, the French had assembled floating batteries with 12 heavy cannons, gunboats, and fireships. The defenders were poised and ready for any kind of British attack.

The French used fireships on the night of June 28th. Wooden ships full of sails and tarred ropes were extremely vulnerable to fire, but the French set fire to the combustible materials in their ships that were floating in the direction of the British ships too soon. Although there were massive explosions and conflagrations, little damage was done to the intended targets.

A painting of the French fireships attempting to block the British advance

A British captain, John Knox, who later published his journal of his wartime experiences in America and who seems to have had a gift for poetic descriptions, said of the scene that night: "They were certainly the grandest fire-works (if I may be allowed to call them so), that can possibly be conceived, every circumstance having contributed to their awful, yet beautiful appearance; the night was serene and calm, there was no light but what the stars produced, and this was eclipsed by the blaze of the floating fires, issuing from all parts, and running almost as quick as thought up the masts and rigging; add to this the solemnity of the sable night, still more obscured by the profuse clouds of smoke, with the firing of the cannon, the bursting of the grenado's, and the crackling of the other combustibles; all which reverberated thro' the air, and the adjacent woods, together with the sonorous shouts, and frequent repetitions of *All's well* from our gallant seamen on the water, afforded a scene, I think, infinitely superior to any adequate description."

Next, Wolfe sent some of his light troops from the island to the village of Beaumont on the south shore of the St. Lawrence, where they ran into some moderate resistance. A manifesto from Wolfe was posted on the Beaumont church's door which read in part, "The formidable sea and land armament which the people of Canada now behold in the heart of their country, is intended by the King, my master, to check the insolence of France, to revenge the insults offered to the British colonies, and totally to deprive the French of their most valuable settlement in North America." It promised not to molest "the industrious peasant, the sacred orders of religion, or the defenceless women and children. . .in their distressful circumstances" and asked for the Canadians to remain neutral in the "great contest" going on between the two crowns. On the other hand, Wolfe's manifesto warned them sternly that if they made the mistake of taking up arms, "they must expect the most fatal consequences; their habitations destroyed, their sacred temples exposed to an exasperated soldiery, their harvest utterly ruined, and the only passage for relief stopped up by a most formidable fleet."

Subsequently, the French sent their floating gun platforms out onto the river to dislodge the British on the shore but were driven off by the broadsides of a British ship. A battery was set up on the shore to prevent a recurrence and an encampment was made. From there, the British could look directly across at the French fortifications on the north shore of the St. Lawrence.

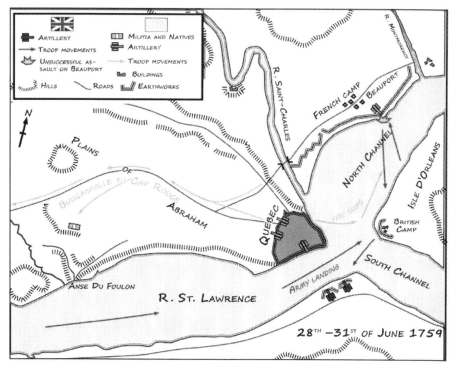

A map of the British positions at the end of June and the unsuccessful attempt to land on the north side above the city on July 31

The Beauport shore Montcalm had heavily fortified east of Québec was exactly where Wolfe had originally been planning to land and to attack the city from by marching inland and around. Now he changed his plans. However, Montcalm had left unfortified the heights at Point Levi on the south side of the St. Lawrence facing and higher than the city. Realizing this, Wolfe sent a force under Monckton to take them. This they did, quickly brushing aside the small number of militia and Indian defenders. After that, the British began building fortifications and hauling cannons up from the river to point them at the city, and despite taking fire from the city's guns, this work was accomplished and the cannons began bombarding the city from there on July 12th. A French attack from across the river later that same day to try to stop the bombardment never made it on account of confusion and bumbling among the volunteers.

Starting with 11 guns, the number of heavy guns pointed at the city was increased to 29 by the end of August, and the British aimed their bombardment not so much at the French gun emplacements and military fortifications but at the buildings of the city, thus destroying the cathedral and many other civilian structures. A Québec parish priest recorded in his diary that during the siege, 40,000 cannonballs and nearly 10,000 bombs fell on the city. At several points, parts of the city were set on fire. In the meantime, throughout August, the British ravaged the surrounding countryside upstream and downstream from Québec, burning an estimated 1,400 farmhouses and barns and killing livestock.

Wolfe's military rationale was that this would provoke Montcalm to emerge from behind the city walls to fight the British in the field, an encounter which Wolfe thought he could win, but Montcalm still refused to take the bait. Under a truce flag, a French soldier admitted, "We do not doubt but you will demolish the town, but we are determined your army will never get footing within its walls." To that, Wolfe replied, "I will be master of Quebec, if I stay here until the latter end of November next." In crafting that response, Wolfe was aware that the successful siege of Louisbourg during the previous year had required several months.

The French may have been determined, but life under siege and constant bombardment was miserable for the inhabitants of Québec. Nevertheless, there was some basis for hope; with the summer drawing to an end and the river soon to be clogged with ice during the long winter months, the British ships and men would have to leave or be trapped. This left some hoping that Québec might survive yet another year without being captured by the British.

The situation offered some hope for the French elsewhere too. The other main British 1759 push – to evict the French from the Champlain Valley – had only been successful up to a point. In July, as the 12,000-man invasion force of British commander-in-chief Jeffery Amherst advanced upon it and put it under siege, Fort Carillon (better known by its subsequent British name, Fort Ticonderoga) was blown up and abandoned by its small French garrison, as was a fort farther north at Crown Point. Per Montcalm's instructions, the French force withdrew toward Montreal to help with defending it if the British chose to attack, but Amherst made no further moves that summer for an attack on Montreal.

In another attempt by Wolfe to draw Montcalm out into the open to fight, British soldiers were sent on July 31st to capture a redoubt in the French defenses near the water's edge. In early July, the British had established a presence on the east side of the Montmorency River, which now divided them from the French defenders, and this was where Wolfe had made his own headquarters. On the 31st, troops under Monckton from across the St. Lawrence were landed on the shore near the redoubt, and some soldiers from the east of the river forded the river at the bottom of the waterfall to meet up with them. Impatient after weeks of inaction, the elite Grenadiers under Monckton launched an attack after the French had withdrawn from the redoubt while waiting for their reinforcements to arrive. In the process, the British had to climb up a steeper slope than expected to get close to the French lines, and a rain storm wet their powder while the French were able to fire at them with the benefit of cover. As night was falling and the tide was starting to come in (which could have prevented the line of retreat by land), Wolfe called a retreat and the surviving soldiers were withdrawn by boat. The battle had been a disaster for the British, who suffered 200 casualties while the victorious French had just 70.

The British were now at their lowest ebb, and recriminations flew among Wolfe and his junior officers about what had gone wrong. Supplies were running short, and when soldiers went out to forage for food, they were harassed by the Canadians and the Indians, sometimes to be found later dead and scalped. Cattle were brought in, but not in sufficient numbers, and military horses were being slaughtered to eat.

Providing some relief for the soldiers' morale, news began to arrive of the British successes against the French at Niagara and in the Champlain Valley, but the siege of Québec seemed to be going nowhere. In spite of the widespread destruction the British artillery bombardments had wreaked, a frontal assault on the city was ruled out as being too dangerous, especially on Québec's key Upper Town, which was too high for the British ships to bring their guns to bear.

Some other kind of plan was needed, and soon, but at this moment, a number of British soldiers and even General Wolfe fell ill from "fluxes and fevers." The bombardment of the city from the heights of Point Levi continued unabated, but further military initiatives were put on hold for several weeks while Wolfe recovered his health. When Wolfe emerged from his sickbed, he presented a plan that involved making another attack at Montmorency, but this plan was rejected by Wolfe's brigadiers because of the already proven strength of the French defenses in that area. They convinced Wolfe that a better option would be to attack from upriver, where they could cut Montcalm's supply lines to the city, force Montcalm to bring his army out to face the British, and prevent a western retreat. After studying the river and rejecting other places as unsuitable, Wolfe chose as the location for the landing the Anse-au-Foulon, a small cove about a mile and a half above the city with a steep path leading up a 50-meter bank. This is now known as "Wolfe's Cove," and the general kept the chosen location secret, even from his own brigadiers, until the last moment.

To execute this plan of attack, Wolfe withdrew his soldiers from the Montmorency River. Leaving behind some as guards, he marched the bulk of his army eight miles up the south side of the river from Point Levi and had them board men-of-war and transport ships that had run the Québec guns. Since the weather was wet, the plan was delayed, but when the soldiers disembarked, it further confused the watching French.

Once again, the soldiers went aboard the ships on the night of September 12th-13th. While other ships and artillery created a diversion east of the city, the first wave of 1800 British soldiers in small boats quietly made their landing. That night, Wolfe dispatched a letter: "I had the honour to inform you today that it is my duty to attack the French army. To the best of my knowledge and ability, I have fixed upon that spot where we can act with most force and are most likely to succeed. If I am mistaken I am sorry for it and must be answerable to His Majesty and the public for the consequences."

A body of French troops was stationed upriver anticipating a possible British landing, but where the British landed, there was stationed only a single company of the militia, and they were surprised and easily dispersed by the vanguard of 24 volunteers who climbed up the steep embankment. The French may also have been deceived since they were expecting a friendly convoy carrying provisions to the city to be coming down river.

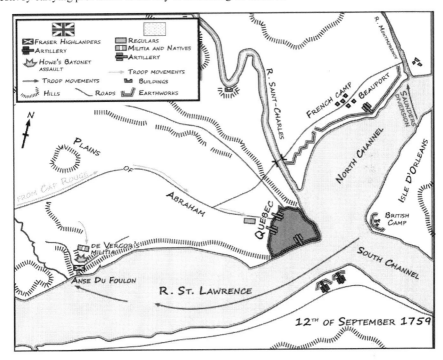

Map of the landing on the night of September 12

By dawn, some 4,400 British soldiers and two pieces of artillery were on the level Plains of Abraham to the west of the city walls. The Plains of Abraham, which would also give the battle its colloquial name, were named for an early settler who had used the land to pasture his cattle. Wolfe detached men to prevent an attack from the French soldiers farther up the river under Bougainville and arrayed the bulk of his men to cover from side to side the entire Québec promontory. With six battalions of foot soldiers plus a detachment of the Louisbourg Grenadiers, the British formed into two lines with 40 or more yards between the units (which led to fewer being hit during the battle.)

Once he recovered from his own surprise, Montcalm mobilized what was probably an equal number of men to confront Wolfe, although about half of them were militia and Indians.

Montcalm's men faced the British with militiamen on the right, regulars in the center, and more regulars and more militiamen on the left. Indians were located in the woods on either side. The French also had three field pieces to fire at the British.

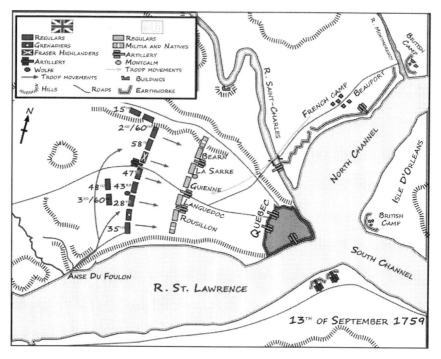

Map of the lines at the start of the battle

At 10:00 a.m. Montcalm, who believed he must act quickly before the British could bring up more troops, ordered an advance in three columns, which was done with loud shouts from his men. The British line, which had been lying down in the grass, rose up and remained firmly in place until after the closing French soldiers fired a salvo (with some confusion by the mixed-together regulars and militia) at a distance of 40 yards. The British infantry held their fire until 20 yards and then fired together with devastating effect, and their second salvo brought the Battle of Québec to a close after scarcely 15 minutes of fighting, with the French either lying dead or dying on the battlefield or beating a retreat back to safety within the city walls. The British soldiers hotly pursued the French soldiers, taking many of them prisoner, and they worked hard to entrench themselves on the ground while bringing up more cannons and ammunition. One British soldier wrote, "The Highlanders pursued them to the very Sally Port of the town. The Highlanders returned towards the main body. When the highlanders were gathered together, they lay'd on a separate attack against a large body of Canadians on our flank that were posted in a small village and a Bush of woods. Here, after a wonderful escape all day, we suffered great loss both in Officers and men but at last drove them under the cover of their cannon which likeways did us considerable loss."

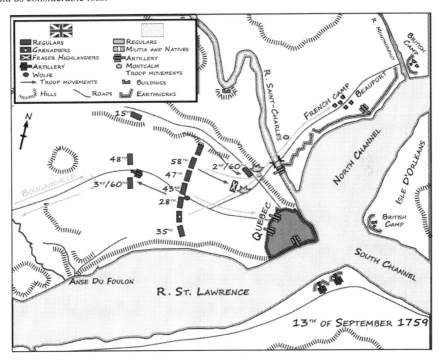

Map of the French retreat

The battle and its aftermath are described in the journal kept by the Sgt. Major of the 40th Regiment's Grenadiers which was published in November 1759 as a pamphlet in Boston:

> "On the 14th [sic] we landed, at break of Day, and immediately attacked and routed the Enemy, taking Possession of a Battery of 4 24-Pounders, and one thirteen Inch Mortar, with but an inconsiderable Loss. We then took Post on the Plains of Abraham, whither M. Montcalm (on hearing that we had landed, for he did not expect us) hasted with his whole Army (consisting of Cavalry as well as Infantry) to give us Battle; about 9 o'Clock; we observed the Enemy marching down towards us in three Columns, at 10 they formed their Line of Battle, which was at least six deep, having their Flanks covered by a thick Wood on each Side,

into which they threw above 3000 Canadians and Indians, who gauled us much; the Regulars then marched briskly up to us, and gave us their first Fire, at about Fifty Yards Distance, which we did not return, as it was General Wolfe's express Orders not to fire till they came within twenty Yards of us --They continued firing by Platoons, advancing in a very regular Manner till they came close up to us, and then the Action became general: In about a Quarter of an Hour the Enemy gave way on all Sides, when a terrible Slaughter ensued from the quick Fire of our Field Pieces and Musquetry with which we pursu'd them to the Walls of the Town, regardless of all excessive heavy Fire from all their Batteries. The Enemy lost in the Engagement, Lieut. Gen. Montcalm, (who was torn to Pieces by our Grape Shot) 2 Brigadier-Generals; one Colonel; 2 Lieutenant-Colonels ; and at least 130 Officers and Men kill'd and 200 taken Prisoners at their very Sally-Ports, of which 58 were Officers. On our Side was killed the brave and never to be forgotten General WOLFE; with 9 Officers, 4 Serjeants and 44 Privates ; wounded, Brigadier-General Monckton , Colonel Carlton, Quarter-Master-General; Major Barre, Adjutant-General; and 50 Other Officers, with 26 Serjeants and 557 privates.-- This Action was the more glorious, as the Enemy were at least 12,000 strong, besides 500 Horse; whereas we, at the utmost, did not consist of above 3500, some of whom did not engage;--for at the Time of the Engagement Colonel Scott was out burning the Country with 1600 Men; Col. Burton was at Point-Levee with 2000 Men; and on the Island of Orleans there were 1500; whereas our whole Army, at our first embarking at Louisbourg, did not exceed 8240 Men.

At Ten o'Clock at Night we surpriz'd their Guard and took Possession of their Grand Hospital, wherein we found between 12 and 1500 Sick and Wounded.

We lay on our Arms all Night, and in the Morning we secured the Bridge of Boats which the Enemy had over Charles River, and possessed ourselves of all, the Posts and Avenues that was or might be of any Consequence leading to the Town, and broke Ground at 100 Yards Distance from the Walls; we likewise got up 12 heavy 24-pounders; six heavy Twelve Pounders, some large Mortars, and the 46 inch Hawitzers, to play upon the Town, and we had been employed three Days, intending to make a Breach, and storm the City Sword in hand, but we were prevented by their beating a Parley, and sending out a Flag of Truce with Articles of Capitulation, and the next Day- being the 17th of September, we took Possession of the City, where we found 250 Pieces of Cannon, a Number of mortars, from 9 to fifteen Inches, Field-Pieces, Hawitzers, &c. with a large Quantity of Artillery-Stores."

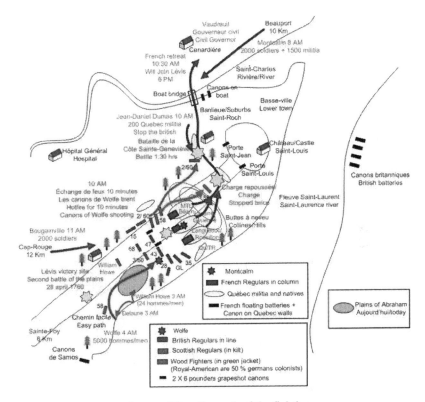

A map of the aftermath of the fighting

The British lost 61 dead and 603 wounded, but the French lost many more, including 370 prisoners. Bouganville arrived at noon from upriver with 2,000 French troops but was too late to help. One of the reasons why this battle is remembered more than many others is that both of the opposing commanders lost their lives in its midst, which gives it a certain macabre romantic fascination. Wolfe was hit several times by gunshots and died rather quickly, his body borne away by 11:00 a.m. to a ship. Montcalm was mortally wounded while riding back inside the city walls, dying the next day from his wounds. Told that he had only a few hours left to live, he said, "So much the better, I am happy that I will not live to see the surrender of Québec."

An illustration of Montcalm leading his men at the battle

A sketch depicting the death of Montcalm

The enduring reputation of Wolfe as a hero has had the assistance of Benjamin West's dramatic 1770 portrait of him dying on the battlefield as a bleeding Christ-like figure surrounded by his officers and men with a squatting Iroquois warrior looking on pensively. Montcalm was buried in the chapel of the Ursuline Convent, and Wolfe's body was buried at a family grave in Greenwich, England. A large sculpture was dedicated to him in Westminster Abbey, showing him dying while being supported by a Grenadier and a Highlander soldier with the figure of Victory descending over him holding a laurel wreath and a palm branch.

Chapter 5: Aftermath of the Battle

The defeat and Montcalm's death left Governor Vaudreuil with a serious quandary about what to do. The dying Montcalm had been sent to for advice, but the mortally wounded commander grimly noted that he was busy attending to his own mortality. Defending the city from within its walls was not a good option because now the British could fire into it from a much closer range; not only did the British have control over the Plains of Abraham, they also now had possession of *les Buttes a Neveu*, a small series of hillocks just east of it that made excellent sites for artillery to be set up. Moreover, the inhabitants of the city were hungry and dispirited from the long siege. Vaudreuil's desire was to attack again, but his officers recommended a retreat by the army and militia to the Jacques Cartier River west of the city, and this is what was done. The commander of the city's garrison, the Chevalier de Ramezay, was left behind to deal with the British. The surrender took place on the morning of September 18th. By the terms of the capitulation, members of the city's garrison were allowed to leave to rejoin the army. The

British agreed not to mistreat the persons and property of the inhabitants and to safeguard the practice of Catholicism until a more permanent peace treaty for the war could happen. The gates of the city were opened and, led by the Grenadiers, the British soldiers, now under Gen. Murray, marched in to take over possession. A Union Jack was raised over the citadel.

News of Wolfe's victory at Québec set off celebrations in Great Britain, as there had also been victories on the European front. At the battle of Minden on August 1st, a combined British-Prussian force had administered a severe defeat to the French, and on August 18th and 19th, a British fleet under Admiral Edward Boscawen had intercepted and destroyed or captured French ships off Portugal heading from the Mediterranean for a port on the Channel to link up with a planned invasion of England or Scotland. On November 20, 1759, in a sea battle off the French coast, the Royal Navy again defeated the French. This battle, the Battle of Quiberon Bay, broke the power of the French fleet and eliminated the danger of a French invasion of Great Britain. 1759 became known as the British "Year of Victories," the *Annus Mirabilis* of 1759.

Montcalm's successor in Canada, by virtue of secret orders he carried, was Brig. Gen. François de Lévis, also a highly experienced military man. Lévis was in Montreal, where he had gone from Québec in August to be closer to the action in case British General Amherst attacked the city, when he received the bad news about Québec. He rushed to rejoin the regrouping French and Canadian militia troops, which he was able to meet up on September 17th at the Jacques Cartier River. Lévis believed that leaving the city had been a serious mistake and ordered the army at once to go back again, but while en route the next day, Lévis learned that Québec had surrendered. Thus, he and his men returned to where they had just come from, and Lévis and Vaudreuil spent the winter in Montreal plotting for a comeback.

François de Lévis

Québec was now controlled by the British and under the governorship of General James

Murray because Monckton, Wolfe's second in command, had been badly wounded in the battle. However, it was a city lying in ruins, and the bishop of Québec, Monseigneur de Pontbriand, described it vividly:

"Quebec has been bombarded and cannonaded for the space of two months; one hundred and eighty houses have been fired by grenades, the remainder shattered by cannon and bombs. The walls, of the thickness of six feet, have not been proof against this; cellars to which well-to-do people had consigned their effects had been burned, forced, and looted, both during and after the siege. The Cathedral has been entirely destroyed. In the Seminary the only habitable part remaining is the kitchen, to which the cure of Quebec has withdrawn in company with his vicar. The Seminary has suffered even greater losses outside the city, for the enemy has burned four of their farms and three considerable mills from which almost their entire revenue is derived. The church of the lower town has been completely demolished; those of the Recollets, the Jesuits and the Seminary are quite unfit for service without most extensive repairs. There is only the Ursuline Church where a decent service can be held, although the English are using it for special services. Both the Ursulines and the Hospitalieres have suffered greatly. They are without means of subsistence, all their lands having been ravaged. Meanwhile, the nuns have managed to lodge themselves after a fashion, after having passed the entire time of the siege in the General Hospital. The Hotel-Dieu is overcrowded, for the English sick are there. The episcopal palace is practically in ruins and does not afford a single habitable room; the cellars have been looted. The houses of the Recollets and the Jesuits are almost as bad; the English have made some slight repairs in order to quarter their troops there. They have billeted their soldiers in those houses which suffered least damage. They drive out from their own houses citizens who, at great expense, have temporarily repaired a room or two, or else so crowd them with the soldiers billeted upon them that nearly all have been obliged to leave this unhappy city. This they are by no means loth to do, for the English refuse to sell except for ready money, and it is well known that the local currency is paper. The priests of the Seminary, the canons and the Jesuits are scattered over what little country has escaped English domination. There are actually people in the city who are without wood for winter, without bread, flour, or meat, and subsisting solely upon a bit of biscuit and a scrap of pork which the English soldiers sell to them out of their rations. Such is the extremity to which our best families are reduced.

"No supplies are to be had from the country, which is in a more deplorable condition than the city itself. All of the cote de Beaupre and the ile d'Orleans had been ravaged before the siege was even over. Farms, dwellings, presbyteries, have been put to the flames. Whatever live stock remained has been seized; those which had been driven into Quebec before the siege, have almost all been consumed by our own troops. In consequence, the poor habitant who returns to his land with his wife and children will be obliged to lodge like a savage. Their crops, only half harvested, will suffer from exposure; likewise their stock. The hiding-places which they had contrived in the forest have been discovered by the enemy, and so the habitant is without goods and chattels, without utensils, and implements for cultivating the soil and felling wood. ... I affirm that this account of our misfortunes is no whit exaggerated, and I entreat our lord bishops and all charitable persons to exert themselves in our behalf."

Québec's inhabitants remained quiet, perhaps shell-shocked, over the winter, and General Murray followed a fairly lenient policy towards the population and put his soldiers to work helping to rebuild the city. At the same time, the fortifications were strengthened.

Murray

Meanwhile, Vaudreuil and Lévis were planning to try to retake the city once fair weather returned. Before the river froze, they were able to get several ships past Québec to request that reinforcements be sent in the spring from France, but the reinforcements never came.

Nonetheless, to retake the city, Lévis assembled an army that was larger – some 7,000 men – than Montcalm had available to oppose Wolfe on September 13th, and by contrast, Murray's defending force had been reduced by troop departures and by deaths from scurvy to fewer than 3,400 men. The battle between the advancing French and the defending British took place on April 28, 1760 at Sainte-Foy, about four miles west of the city walls. Another set piece battle in the European manner, this was a longer and much harder fought battle with higher casualties on both sides than the one that had been fought on the Plains of Abraham half a year earlier. The

French ultimately prevailed in this battle, with the British soldiers abandoning their guns and retreating back to the city. Lévis now put Québec under siege, but the British were saved by the timely arrival of ships carrying reinforcements for them.

The Battle of Sainte-Foy was the last major battle in the French & Indian War. As British forces in overwhelming numbers converged on Montreal from three directions – up the St. Lawrence from Québec City on the east, up the Richelieu River from Lake Champlain from the south, and along the St. Lawrence from Lake Ontario in the west -- Vaudreuil and Lévis, now left with only several thousand soldiers, surrendered Montreal on September 8, 1760.

The French made one final attempt to salvage something that they could use as a bargaining chip in the peace negotiations, especially with regards to fishing rights. In June 1762, a small naval force from France slipped by the British blockade, surprised the garrison at St. John's, Newfoundland, and forced its capitulation. In September, the British landed a force to take it back, and on September 15th, in the Battle of Signal Hill a few miles north of St. John's, the British defeated the French. The Seven Years War was basically over.

Chapter 6: The Legacy of the Battle and the War

A map of British and Spanish gains at the end of the war

The Treaty of Paris signed on February 10, 1763 officially ended the Seven Years War (and the French & Indian War in North America), and France was the big loser. Given a choice of taking back its small sugar plantation islands of Guadalupe and Martinique in the Caribbean that had been captured by Britain or all of Canada, it chose the former. Sugar was highly profitable for the French Crown, while Canada had long run a deficit. Havana, captured by the British in 1762, was returned to Spain, France's ally, and the Louisiana Territory of New France west of the Mississippi River was transferred to the control of Spain. On the other hand, in the diplomatic give and take, Spain was forced to give up Florida to Great Britain, and Minorca, captured by the French early in the war, was returned to Great Britain.

In North America, France received one small concession in the treaty. In order to furnish the French fishermen, who had long fished on the banks off Newfoundland, with an onshore place to dry their fish, France was allowed to keep the tiny islands of St. Pierre and Miquelon. In one of the oddest geographical footnotes of the era, those two islands southwest of Newfoundland are still today part of France.

As Fred Anderson has observed in his monumental history of the conflict, the Treaty of Paris in 1763 was a "phenomenal diplomatic coup" for Great Britain. Britain's American colonists now no longer had to fear what they had dreaded for 150 years: the French and their Indian allies coming down on them from Canada and bearing off scalps and captives. The contested Ohio territory was now open to American land speculators and white settlers (although actually taking control of it would require more combat with the Indians through the War of 1812).

However, in winning the war in North America, the British Crown had run up an enormous debt of over one million pounds sterling, and the British citizenry were already heavily taxed. Quite understandably, since the expensive war in North America had been fought and won in large part for the benefit of the American colonists, the British government thought they ought to help shoulder the financial burden. The British government was also upset that during the war, some of the American colonists had engaged in trade with the French islands in the Caribbean. This was not only a direct violation of imperialist mercantilist laws but also, in the wartime context, almost treasonous conduct., and they were determined to crack down on it. Moreover, a pan-Indian uprising in the Midwest, Pontiac's Rebellion, started in May 1763 and convinced the British that they would have to maintain an ongoing military presence in the colonies to keep the whites and the Indians apart. The continuing defense of the colonists in this way would impose an additional financial burden.

Moreover, the 13 colonies were relatively untaxed by Great Britain compared to England, Scotland, and Wales, and no member of Parliament represented the colonies, so Parliament could increase taxes on the colonies without a great deal of Parliamentary opposition or backlash among British citizens. Of course, this last fact, while convenient for Parliament, created a great deal of ill will in the 13 colonies. Many colonists believed that Parliament had no right to raise taxes when the colonies had no representation in Parliament, and they pointed to the fact that the King of England had long since surrendered any claim to raise taxes without the consent of the people's representatives in Parliament. A Parliament without a single American member, the colonists' argued, could no more legally raise taxes on them than the King could on British citizens. Taxation without representation was, in the colonists' view, a violation of their rights as Englishmen.

One of the oft forgotten aspects of the British taxes on the colonies in the 1760s is that they were not terribly repressive. In fact, some of the British measures that were opposed by the colonists actually lowered the prices colonists paid for imported goods (including the Tea Act of 1773). The Sugar Act of 1764 was one of the British "taxes" that ostensibly lowered the price of imported goods because it lowered the duty on molasses from six pence to three, thereby replacing the duty imposed by the Molasses Act of 1733. New England merchants, who imported barrels of molasses from the West Indies for the manufacture of rum, had not protested the original Molasses Act of 1733's six pence duty 30 years earlier.

In addition to taxes, two other post-French & Indian War actions by Britain incensed many colonists in the run-up to the Revolutionary War and ultimately contributed to the outbreak of hostilities in 1775. In 1763, the government issued a proclamation that ran a line of demarcation from north to south down the heights of the Appalachian Mountains. To prevent further conflict with the Indians and to keep the colonists where they could be more easily controlled, the colonists were ordered to stay east of the line and away from the Indians who were living to the west of it. This action greatly angered colonial land speculators – George Washington was one of them – and land-hungry settlers from the increasingly crowded colonies along the eastern seaboard.

The second British action came in 1774, when the Québec Act set up a permanent colonial government for the region captured from France in 1763. It restored privileges to the Catholic religion, particularly angering colonists of Puritan-stock in New England, and the geographical jurisdiction of the Québec was extended into the Great Lakes and Midwest, another blow to American colonial hopes for expansion into those war-acquired territories.

At the same time, following the surrender of Québec in 1759 and the surrender of Montreal in 1760, British military rulers had, through lenient policies, won at least at a grudging acceptance from the local populations. One of the first actions of the Continental Congress after the battles of Lexington and Concord was to send soldiers to take Canada from the British, and Québec was again besieged, this time by colonists led by Benedict Arnold. However, this time, a combination of a smallpox epidemic among the American soldiers and resistance from the British soldiers and Canadian militias now working together defeated the attempt.

France eventually entered into an alliance with the United States after the American victory at

Saratoga, New York in October 1777. As a way to get back at Great Britain for its losses during the Seven Years War, France sent money and soldiers to help support Washington's ragged Continentals, but France would not benefit materially from being on the winning side of this war. No parts of Canada were returned to it, and what it acquired instead was a large debt of its own. That debt would help bring about the French Revolution in 1789.

Not all of the American colonists had supported independence; in fact, up to a third of them in some locations were Loyalists. Many took up arms against other Americans alongside the British, and other persecuted Loyalists were assisted by the British and set up as pioneers in parts of Canada, including parts of Québec. A number of the former slaves of the colonists also found refuge in Canada.

Canada was divided governmentally in 1791, with Québec proper becoming "Lower Canada" and the area which is now Ontario becoming "Upper Canada." Lower Canada maintained a Francophone majority, but a steady stream of English-speaking and other types of settlers arriving in the rest of Canada during the 19th century rendered the Francophone population a minority overall.

Still, the events of the 18th century continue to influence Québec today. Even now, the Québec automobile license plates features the motto "Je me souviens," meaning "I remember." This refers to what the descendants of the French colonists (Québécois) considered to have been "The Conquest," when the British took over Canada from what is rightfully theirs. Many if not all Francophones in Quebec are "sovereigntists" who feel that their culture has not been sufficiently respected and that they have been discriminated against as a minority within English-dominated Canada since 1763. Many of them would like to see Québec leave Canada and become a separate country. When the separatist Parti Québécois (PQ) was elected to govern the province, they organized two referendums on Québec independence (1980 and 1995), both of which fell short of passage.

What the future holds for the province of Québec is unclear. The city of Québec is today a metropolis of over 500,000 people, one that is very proud of its spectacular location overlooking the St. Lawrence River and its prodigious historical heritage. Québec welcomes tourists from all over the world who come to walk its old narrow, cobblestoned European-style streets and visit the fortifications and battlegrounds. Québec's historical district has been declared a UNESCO World Heritage site, and the Winter Carnival and Saint-Jean-Baptiste Day, Québec's national holiday, are especially big draws for visitors.

As with other important battles in history, historians, military gamers, and armchair generals have debated whether the Battle of Québec could have gone differently. Much of the conjecture centers around Montcalm; what if Montcalm had not attacked the British so hastily – and fatefully – on the Plains of Abraham? What if Bouganville had arrived on the scene more quickly and had squeezed the British between his forces and Montcalm's? What if Montcalm had not been killed? There is also the question of whether an altered outcome of events that happened elsewhere in the Seven Years War might have saved Québec in 1759 by permitting the flow of needed men and supplies to the besieged city.

Either way, it is hard to imagine that Québec could have avoided being besieged by an even larger British forces again during the following year. One way or another, a battle for Québec was going to be an historical turning point, with the odds favoring the British to emerge as the victors.

Bibliography

A Journal of the Expedition up the River St. Lawrence; Containing a True and Most Particular Account of the Transactions of the Fleet and Army Under the Command of Admiral Saunders and General Wolfe, from the Time of Their Embarkation at Louisbourg 'Til After the Surrender of Quebeck. Boston: Printed and sold by Fowle and Draper, 1759.

Anderson, Fred. *Crucible of War: The Seven Years' War and the Fate of Empire in British North America, 1754-1766*. New York: Vintage, 2001.

"Battles of 1759 and 1760." *The National Battlefield Commission: Plains of Abraham*, http://bataille.ccbn-nbc.gc.ca/en/.

"Fortifications of Québec National Historic Site of Canada." *Parks Canada*, http://www.pc.gc.ca/eng/lhn-nhs/qc/fortifications/natcul/natcul1.aspx.

Halpenny, Francess G., and Jean Hamelin, eds. *Dictionary of Canadian Biography*. Toronto: University of Toronto Press, 1988.

Howard, Michael. *War in European History*. Oxford: Oxford University Press, 2009.

Knox, John. *An Historical Journal of the Campaigns in North-America, for the Years 1757, 1758, 1759, and 1760*. London: Printed for the author, and sold by W. Johnston ... and J. Dodsley, 1769.

Nester, William R. *The Great Frontier War: Britain, France, and the Imperial Struggle for North America, 1607-1755*. Westport, Conn.: Praeger Publishers, 2000.

Parkman, Francis. *Montcalm and Wolfe*. Vol. 2. Boston: Little, Brown, 1884.

Sulte, Benjamin, C. E. Fryer, and Laurent-Olivier David. *A History of Quebec: Its Resources and People: Illustrated*. Vol. 1. Montreal: Canada History Co., 1908.

Made in the USA
Middletown, DE
21 February 2017